*"Here's How To Use the Money You
Already Earn To
Dump Your Student Debt Fast..."*

School Loans
Gone!

A Step-By-Step System For Turbo-Charging
Your Current Income, Saving Thousands of
Dollars in Interest Payments, and Becoming
Completely Student Loan Free Years Ahead
of Schedule.

Christopher T. Lawson, CRPC

ISBN: 1480288276
ISBN-13: 978-1480288270

2

Dedication

To the 37 million Americans suffering from student loan debt and my brilliant and generous sister Megan, without whom this book would not have been possible.

Introduction

Congratulations! You Worked Hard For Your Education...

It took many years to complete and now you are considered among the most educated and respected members of our society. Unfortunately, you also have a mountain of student loan debt to show for it.

If you're like most of our clients, somewhere in the back of your head you remember the brief student loan exit interview where they mentioned something about paying-off your student loan debt the way that the lenders recommend and that it will take about 30 years to accomplish. The small print you may not remember is that this method of repayment would have the typical borrower with a $100,000 student loan balance paying over $160,000 in interest payments on top of the original loans assuming an 8% interest rate. That's 360 monthly payments of $733.76, a full 30 years of stressing over debt, pinching pennies, skipping vacations and worrying about how you are going to save for your own retirement or send your kids to college. I wrote this book to show you that there is a better way.

The system you are about to learn is the result of over 18 years of helping families save, invest and plan for their financial futures. This how-to manual combines all of the proven tools, strategies and skills accumulated over this 18 year period to one sole purpose; helping college graduates and highly educated professionals buried in student loans to get organized, gain clarity, restore peace of mind, and pay off student loan debt faster than they ever thought possible while saving thousands of dollars in the process. And to accomplish all of this with the money they are already earning.

I have done extensive personal interviews (over 120 to date) and along with my team have created financial plans for clients with undergraduate degrees, doctors, lawyers, PhD's, MBA's, and many other highly educated professionals. Before we started working together, many of these professionals had over $100,000 in student loans that they had been paying on for years. In the course of our work we have compiled a list of the biggest fears and frustrations our clients and interviewees have had with respect to their outstanding student loans. Do you share any of them?

- I feel like I worked hard for my education and hard in my job and when I look at the amount I still owe in student loans, I feel like I didn't get anything for it.

- I have been paying on my loans for years and it seems like the balances haven't gone down at all.

- I feel like I'm just barely treading water with all of the student loan debt I'm carrying waiting for the next wave to hit.

- My student loan payment is the biggest bill we have besides the rent. We could have a decent sized house for what I pay in student loan payments each month.

- I'm not comfortable with the level of debt I'm carrying. I'm constantly stressed out because it's so large and anytime I have to deal with it I just freeze. I just feel like I'm in denial and I want to stick my head in the sand and hope it will all go away.

- I feel like I can't do other things because of this student loan debt. It is such a burden and I feel like it took away my choices because all of my effort has to go toward paying-off the debt.

- I'm afraid that I will never be able to buy a house, a new car, send my kids to college or retire because of these loans.

- I'm afraid that in 30 years I will want to retire but will still be paying on these loans. I feel like I could be paying these loans for the rest of my life and my kids could even end up paying them through my estate after I'm gone.

- The financial stress I'm under because of the loans has also put stress on my marriage.

In this how-to manual we are going to reveal the step-by-step School Loans Gone system that will allow you to pay off all of your student loan debt faster than you ever thought possible, save thousands of dollars in interest payments, and shave years or even decades off your pay off schedule.

If you have any outstanding student loan debt, this system is for you. And the more debt you have, the better it will work.

Our promise to you: if you apply this system to your financial life and give it even a fraction of the effort and attention that you gave to your education, you will discover how to dramatically accelerate your student loan pay off schedule and save thousands of dollars in interest payments. Our clients who use this system on average shave a minimum of 11 years off their pay-off schedule and save at least $27,000 in interest payments.

NOTE: Each section begins with an actual quote from a client regarding an issue we helped them with through the School Loans Gone system.

Who is Christopher T. Lawson, CRPC, and Why Did He Write This Book?

Hi, my name is Chris Lawson and I've been active in the financial services industry for over 18 years as a private wealth manager, Chartered Retirement Planning Counselor, seminar leader, and educator. Since 2010, I've devoted my career to helping those who suffer under a crippling amount of student loan debt.

After seeing more and more of my planning clients suffering along with nearly 37 million other Americans because of their student loan debt, I developed the system you are about to learn in these pages. This system has helped hundreds of clients just like you to accelerate their student loan pay off and get back to enjoying their lives.

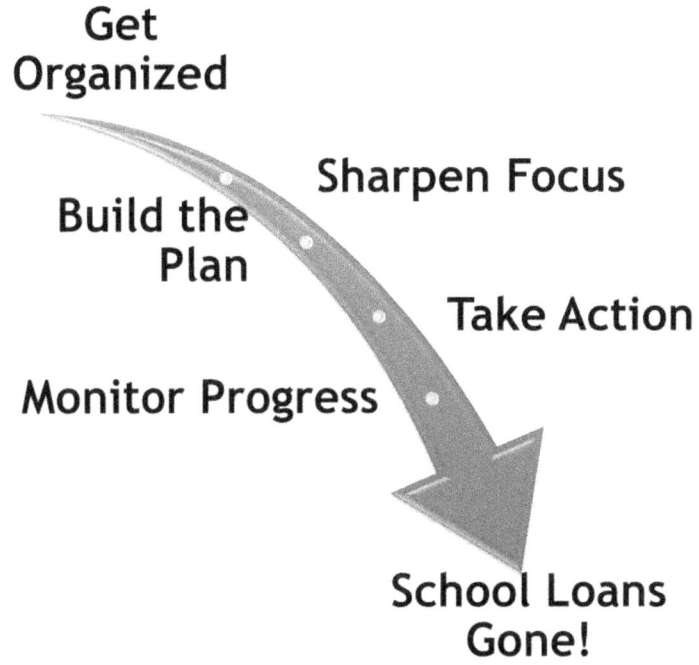

Table of Contents

Chapter 1: Get Organized

Laying the Foundation

"I would like to have a clear path to paying off my student loans and doing the other things I want to do."

Laying the foundation is the first step toward rapidly paying off your student loan debt and beginning to build real wealth in your life. If you do a thorough job of completing all of the actions in this chapter, you will be well on your way to expanding your choices and options and it will make the rest of this program a breeze for you.

If you don't take this chapter seriously, it will require you to backtrack later on in the program which will significantly slow your progress and increase your frustration and the chances that you will not complete the program and miss out on saving thousands of dollars and shaving years off your pay off schedule.

Think of Your Student Loan Debt as a Jigsaw Puzzle

"I'm in denial, my head is stuck in the sand and I don't even want to think about my student loans."

Most people I work with have been carrying their student loan debt for years and a very common reaction to the entire situation is to pile the bills into a box, make the minimum payments and try to forget about it. In the short term this strategy seems to work but in the long term that gnawing lump of anxiety in the pit of your stomach continues to grow because in the back of your mind you know that you aren't in control and the situation is not going away for many years.

Any good financial plan starts with gathering data. Data is

the raw unprocessed material of your financial life. Don't let the jargon scare you. I like to describe this process as if you were going to put together a jigsaw puzzle. The first thing you would do is open the box and dump the pieces out on the table. Then you would turn the pieces over so you could see the colors and although you may not count each piece, you would get an overall feel for whether or not the pieces on the table represented the total number listed on the box.

This is exactly the same process we will follow for your student loan debt. We want to pull out all of your financial documents and get them in one place. Don't worry about what to do with them yet, this step is simply to gather all of the pieces of your financial life into one place so we can see the whole financial picture and begin putting the puzzle together in the proper way.

Gathering the Pieces of the Puzzle

"My lifestyle is important and I don't want to work more and sacrifice that."

All you have to do in this step is gather all of your financial documents along with the monthly statements from each of your debts. Using the Document Checklist in Chapter 7 will be a tremendous help in completing this step. Many of these documents are now online. If so, print out a copy so you can have all the information you need in one place for the steps we will take in Chapter 2.

How to find the documents you will need:

Federal Student Loans

Printing the on-line statements you receive or gathering your paper monthly statements is the best way to obtain the data you need for your Federal student loans. However, if you are not sure that you have everything you need you can always check the National Student Loan Data System for information on your Federal student loans. The National Student Loan Data System (NSLDS) www.nslds.ed.gov is the U.S. Department of Education's central database for student aid and it contains information on all of your Title IV loans and grants including: amounts, outstanding balances, loan status, and disbursements.

You can also contact the Federal Student Aid Information Center (FSAIC). Their toll-free number is 1-800-4-FED-AID or 1-800-433-3243. They have access to the federal database and can answer questions and provide you with information about your federal student loans.

As a last resort, your school's financial aid department will also have information on your student loans.

Private Student Loans

The best way to obtain your private student loan information is from the statements you receive from your lender either online or through snail mail.

You can also contact your school's financial aid department for information on your student loans.

What to do Right Now

"I feel like I'm treading water waiting for the next wave to hit."

Let's keep this simple, here's what to do right now to get started:

Flip forward to the Document Checklist in chapter 7 and copy it or go to our website at www.FinancialEvolutionGroup.com and print out a PDF version. Spend the next 30 minutes locating each of the documents listed on this checklist and placing a checkmark next to each of the documents as you place them in a single pile on top of your desk or kitchen table.

If you need more time, stop at 30 minutes anyway, take a short 10-15 minute break and come back refreshed. If you are super organized this step will be a snap. If you are like many people, this step may take a little longer. Just remember, take your time and don't get frustrated by this process. You have everything you need and it's just a matter of finding it and putting it all into one place.

You will know you have done this right if each of the lines on this checklist has a checkmark next to it when you are done. If any of the lines are still blank when you have finished, make sure that the item on the list is applicable to you and if so review this chapter for instructions on how to locate the missing documents. If the blank lines refer to documents that don't apply to you, simply ignore them.

Well done! The first foundation step is now done and you are well on your way to saving thousands of dollars on your student loan interest payments and shaving years off of your repayment schedule. You are building momentum and you should feel great about your progress.

Chapter 1 Action Steps Review

- Print out the Document Checklist in Chapter 7.

- Locate each of the documents on the list.

- Place each document in a pile on your desk or kitchen table.

- Place a checkmark next to each document as you place it on the pile.

Print out document checklist from www.FinancialEvolutionGroup.com or copy it from chapter 7.

Locate each document on the list.

Place each document in a pile.

Place a checkmark on the checklist next to each document as it is added to the pile.

Chapter 2: Sharpen Your Focus

Now it's Time to Gain Some Clarity

"My student loan debt took away my choices and options."

This is the revealing step where you plug the information gathered in chapter 1 into the worksheets that will completely transform the way you look at your financial life forever. Once you have all of your financial information in the right format, you can begin to see ways to move things around, become more efficient with your finances and gain enormous leverage in accelerating the payoff of all of your debt and most importantly, your student loans.

This may seem like a long chapter but keep in mind that all we are doing here is taking the information you gathered in the last chapter and transferring it into a new format, that's it!

Be sure and treat this chapter seriously because without a clear visual framework to view your financial information you will simply remain in a fog unable to see any options or choices for improving your financial situation and doing all of the other things you really want to do with your life.

You Inc. How to Run Your Financial Life like a Successful Company

"I don't feel like I have the freedom to do anything else besides what I'm doing because I have to earn so much to pay back my loans."

A big part of the value that financial planners provide for their clients is the ability to take all of the seemingly unconnected financial data from them and re-present it to them in a clear, crisp, easy to read manner. It's amazing how differently you are able to see the exact same information when it is presented in a different way. And this new clarity allows you to make better, more confident decisions with respect to your financial life.

This is how publicly traded companies operate. Do to the high levels of financial scrutiny a publicly traded company receives from shareholders, internal and external auditors, ratings agencies, creditors, and potential investors, they are constantly on their toes and obligated to keep perfect and transparent financial records. These records also allow them to monitor the financial health of their operations, squeeze more value out of every dollar, and find ways to make more money.

In this chapter you are going to learn how to run your financial life like a successful financial corporation (an honest, successful corporation). Don't worry, you will be amazed by how easy this process is and the power and control over your finances that results will simply amaze you.

Let's go back to our puzzle analogy for a moment. In this chapter what we will be doing with your financial data is similar to grouping the pieces of the puzzle with the same colors and setting aside the pieces with the flat edges that will eventually become the border for the picture.

Financial clarity is a very counter intuitive subject. When I work with clients to get clear on their financial situation often they are nervous to see what they will find when all of the stones have been uncovered. But when they see all of the information in one place for the very first time something almost magical happens. Almost without exception they say something like, "Wow, that's not as bad as I thought." The financial fog they had been in burns away and a new clarity and focus arises.

In this chapter we will be constructing the documents that professional corporations use to show you visually how money is moving through your life right now and what will happen if you keep doing what you are doing. In the next chapter we will look at ways to improve your situation.

The Income Statement (Spending Plan)

The Income Statement is an analysis of your income and expenses. This document will allow you to see how money flows into your life as income (your job and all other sources of money moving into your life) and how it flows out of your life through your expenses (all of the things you spend money on).

This is a very powerful tool and all we are going to do in this chapter is build it. In the next chapter we will analyze and turbocharge your Income statement and you will see the positive results of these shifts immediately.

The Balance Sheet (Net Worth Statement)

The Balance Sheet tells you what your net worth is. When you take all of the items in your life that have financial value (Assets) and subtract all of the items in your life that you owe (Liabilities) what you are left with is your net worth. This is a vitally important document that gives you a snapshot of where you stand financially at this particular moment in time.

The Debt Pay Off Order Spreadsheet

The Debt Pay Off Order Spreadsheet is the document where you will enter the critical information about all of your debts, school loans, credit cards, your mortgage, anything that you owe that has an outstanding balance. The purpose of this document is to gain clarity on what you owe and to have it presented for you in a format that will allow you to see exactly what order your debts should be paid off in to gain you the most momentum and provide the most rapid pay off.

What to do Right Now

"Our student loan payment is the biggest bill we have besides the rent."

Let's begin by filling in the data for the Income Statement. From the pile of financial documents you created in Chapter 1, pull out the following documents and set them aside:

- CHECKBOOK REGISTER, CHECK STUBS, OR CHECK COPIES FOR ALL BANK ACCOUNTS

- SAVINGS AND CHECKING ACCOUNT STATEMENTS FOR ALL ACCOUNTS (LAST 3 MONTHS TO GET A FEEL FOR THE TREND, ONE MONTH ALONE COULD BE UNUSUALLY HIGH OR LOW

- CREDIT CARD STATEMENTS

- PAY STUB FROM YOUR EMPLOYER(S)

- PENSION, DISABILITY / SOCIAL SECURITY, OF RETIREMENT INCOME STATEMENTS

- ALIMONY OR CHILD SUPPORT INFORMATION

Next, print out the "Income Statement (Spending Plan Spreadsheet)" from Chapter 7.

Now complete the bottom right hand box titled "Income" on the Income Statement (Spending Plan Spreadsheet) using the documents from above.

After you have entered all sources of income in the spreadsheet, it's now time to move over to your expenses. The easiest way to complete this task is to use your reports from Quicken or Microsoft money to fill in each of the categories listed on the Income Statement (Spending Plan Spreadsheet). If you don't use either of these programs it is easiest to take out a sheet of paper or legal pad and begin listing all of the things you have spent money on in the last month using your checkbook register, check stubs, checking account statements, and Credit card statements.

Place a header on a new column for each new category; use the categories on the Income Statement (Spending Plan Worksheet) as a guide for the column headers. Once you have gone through all of the ways you spend money for the month, add up each category and add the total to the corresponding category on the spreadsheet.

Once all of your income and expenses have been entered on the spreadsheet simply total up the numbers and obtain your "Monthly Income Availability" found in the bottom right-hand side of the spreadsheet.

Congratulations! You are all done with this document for now. In the next chapter we will analyze the results and look for ways to maximize your numbers.

Now we want to move over to the Balance Sheet (Net Worth Statement). From the pile of financial documents you created in Chapter 1, pull out the following documents and set them aside:

- CURRENT MORTGAGE STATEMENTS FOR ALL REAL ESTATE

- FINANCIAL STATEMENTS

- INVESTMENT STATEMENTS (PERSONAL)

- 401(K) STATEMENTS

- ESOP

- DEFERRED COMPENSATION

- COLLEGE SAVINGS ACCOUNT (STATEMENTS)

- Auto / RV Statement

- Other Liabilities (credit, equity line)

- Living Expenses Projections or Budget

- (Quicken, Excel Reports)

- Checkbook Register, Check Stubs, or Check Copies for All Bank Accounts

- Credit Card Statements

- Savings and Checking Account statements for all accounts (last 3 months to get a feel for the trend, one month alone could be unusually high or low)

- Student loan statements (all)

- Personal loan information (can be a handwritten list of anything else you owe)

Next, print out the Balance Sheet (Net Worth Statement) from chapter 7.

Now complete this entire worksheet with the documents from above. Begin with all of your assets in the left column of the worksheet. Use the headings to guide you to the appropriate document in your pile to obtain the numbers you need. If you have additional assets that don't correspond to a heading, simply place it on the worksheet in the "other" category.

After you have completed the assets column move over to the Liabilities column. Here you will list all of the items that create and expense or cash outflow. This is where you list everything in your life that you owe money on. From your student loans to your home, car or credit cards.

Once you have completed the liability section now it's time

to calculate your net worth. Total up your assets and liabilities and then subtract the total of your liabilities from the total of the assets.

The result may be a bit surprising and it's not at all unusual for people with large student loan balances to find that they have a negative net worth. Don't worry about whatever shows up for now. Just fill in the worksheets and add up the totals. We will focus on improving your numbers in the next chapter. Remember, take baby steps to start.

Some additional notes as you complete your Balance Sheet:

- Don't be too generous with assets just to make your situation look better. Clear accurate numbers will be much more helpful to you as you track your progress and build momentum. For example, if you spent $5,000 on clothes that's not what they would be worth if you sold them. Think about what you would be able to get for them at a garage sale or on Craigslist.org, 10% to 20% tops.

- Think of assets as something that bring in income or can be converted to cash to feed you.

- Think of liabilities as something that siphons wealth out of your life or eats you. These items cause an expense or cash outflow.

- Under this definition think very carefully about what truly is an asset. Is that living room set going to feed you? Probably not and if you sold it you wouldn't get anywhere near the value you paid for it. Here's a brief list of "assets" that you probably won't sell anyway and in most cases have little resale value:

    o Furniture

- Tools
- Appliances
- Jewelry
- Clothing
- Electronics
- Sports equipment

- Lump these items together and put a set number of $1,500 max for them and move on.

Next, print out the Debt Pay Off Order Spreadsheet from chapter 7.

This part will be easy because you did most of the leg work when you completed your Balance Sheet.

1. Write the name of each loan / debt in column 1.

2. Write the total balance owed in column 2.

3. Write the monthly minimum payment of each loan / debt in column 3.

4. Divide the total balance owed by the monthly minimum payment and put the answer in column 4.

5. Prioritize pay-off starting with the lowest division answer as the first loan / debt to pay off (#1). Input this number in column 5 and continue numbering each subsequent debt in ascending order.

Congratulations! You have now completed your financial documents and you are now ready to begin the analysis process in the next chapter where we figure out how to pay off your debts fast. Don't worry it sounds more complicated than it is, just follow the baby steps as we lay them out for you.

What to look for as you complete the steps in Chapter 2 to make sure you are on the right track

As you begin to implement the action steps listed in the following section, here's what to watch for to make sure that that you are on the right track:

- All of the blanks in each of the forms are completed with numbers or an N/A for items that are not applicable.

- Totals on each spreadsheet should be fairly close to what you would estimate. For example, if you know that your income is in a certain range and your expenses are in a certain range, any number you come up with on the worksheet that falls outside of this range would be a red flag to go back and double check the numbers on your financial documents.

- If there are any financial documents that you gathered in Chapter 1 that you didn't use for the completing of the worksheets in Chapter 2, this may be a red flag that there is an area that you missed on one of the worksheets.

- Once you get all of your information neatly organized and recorded in the worksheets you should feel a substantial relief as a new clarity of your financial picture becomes evident.

- Many clients report that they are even able to see ways that they can improve their situation from the new perspective these worksheets create for them.

Chapter 2 Action Steps Review

- Take out the documents from your financial document pile that relate to your income and expenses.

- Print the "Income Statement (Spending Plan)" spreadsheet from Chapter 7.

- Fill in the blanks on the spreadsheet and add the column totals.

- Take the documents out of the financial documents pile that relate to your assets (Investments) and liabilities (Debts).

- Print the "Balance Sheet (Net Worth Statement)" spreadsheet from Chapter 7.

- Fill in the blanks on the spreadsheet and add the column totals.

- Review once more the documents that pertain to your liabilities (Debts).

- Print the "Debt Pay Off Order" spreadsheet from Chapter 7.

- Fill in the blanks on this spreadsheet and calculate the required totals as listed.

- Remove income and expense documents from financial document pile.

- Copy the "Income Statement (Spending Plan) spreadsheet from chapter 7 or print PDF from website www.financialevolutiongroup.com.

- Fill in blanks on Income Statement spreadsheet and add column totals.

- Remove assets and liabilities documents from financial document pile.

- Copy the "Balance Sheet (Net Worth Statement)" spreadsheet from chapter 7 or print PDF from website.

- Fill in blanks on the Balance Sheet spreadsheet and add column totals.

- Go back to the documents that pertain to your liabilities (debts).

- Copy the "Debt Pay Off Order" spreadsheet from chapter 7 or print the PDF from website.

- Fill in the blanks on the Debt Pay Off Order spreadsheet and calculate totals.

Chapter 3: Build Your Plan

What Napoleon Bonaparte Would have Done if He had Student Loan Debt

"I've been paying for 7 years non-stop and have only paid down $2,000."

This chapter is all about the power of focus. Napoleon Bonaparte has been recognized as one of history's most brilliant military strategists largely because he was able to focus his armies' power and deliver dramatic military victories. We will borrow one of Napoleon's most powerful strategies and apply it to your student loan debt. The goal of this chapter is simple, to find a minimum of $200.00 in your spending plan and allocate it toward your student loans in a specific way. If you follow the simple steps in this chapter you will learn how to find a minimum of $200.00 extra dollars in your spending plan each month and how to turn that $200.00 into a result like this:

One client with $75,000 of student loan debt and an average 3.75% interest rate on their loans was able to shave 9.3 years and $15,833 in interest payments.

Don't skip over this powerful information because if you fail to apply these steps, you could end up paying on your student loans for an extra decade and lose thousands of hard earned dollars to unnecessary interest payments.

The benefits of financial focus

"I'm stressed out because I can only pay the minimums each month."

Throughout history there have been examples of how

concentration of effort and resources has been effective in achieving goals. The military strategies of Napoleon Bonaparte are a good example of this. One of his favorites was the strategy of central position which was used effectively many times to secure decisive victories. This strategy required his army to marshal forces and use the bulk of their troops as a unified front to penetrate enemy concentrations in order to prevent them from uniting. Once the enemy forces were divided it was just a matter of time until each of the divided factions was surrounded and defeated.

This exact same strategy can work for your money. If you use a spending plan to concentrate your financial resources in the manner outlined here, you will begin to see your loan balances go down rapidly. As the momentum builds you also get an added psychological benefit because once you can see that you are making progress instead of constantly feeling like all of the money you have been paying is going into a black hole, it becomes a game to see how much you can maximize your spending plan to wipe out bigger and bigger chunks of your debt each month.

Going back to our puzzle analogy, this step is like looking at the box to see the picture you are trying to replicate and deciding which color groups or area of the puzzle you want to start on first.

See the chart on the next page for the power of finding additional money in your spending plan and applying it strategically to pay off debt.

					Debt Pay-Off Order				
Name of Debt	Total Balance	Monthly Minimum Payment	Interest Rate	Pay-Off Priority	Pay-off info if you keep doing what you are doing	Pay-Off info $0 FFP*	Pay-Off info $200 FFP*	Pay-Off info $500 FFP*	Pay-Off info $1,000 FFP*
Visa	$4,500.00	$90.00	14.24%	1	Jan-18	Jan-18	Feb-13	May-12	Jan-12
ACS	$8,500.00	$75.00	6.50%	2	May-26	Apr-21	Jan-15	May-13	Aug-12
Perkins Loan	$23,000.00	$180.00	5.00%	3	Nov-26	Jan-24	Mar-18	Aug-15	Jan-14
Sallie Mae	$98,000.00	$780.00	6.80%	4	Jan-30	Nov-27	Jan-24	Nov-20	Feb-18
				Years to Total Debt Freedom	18.4	16.3	12.4	9.3	6.5
				Total Interest Paid	($90,783.00)	($85,213.00)	($62,347.00)	($45,355.00)	($31,343.00)

* Using rapid pay off plan

As you can see from the chart above, something as simple as finding an additional $200 per month in this client's spending plan can result in a savings of 6 years and $28,446 in interest payments. If they were able to find an additional $500 per month they would save 9.1 years and $45,438 in interest payments. The final column illustrates an ambitious but achievable result for many families that apply discipline. The result of finding an additional $1,000 in the monthly spending plan has this client paying off all debt including a credit card (a total of $134,000 in debt) in six and a half years and saving $59,450 in interest payments!

As you can see, time spent on the following simple exercises will produce an awesome return on your investment so let's get started.

What to Do Right Now

"I don't want to be in debt for the rest of my life but I don't see a way out."

Now you've reached the point where you are ready to kick your student loan debt repayment into hyper drive. You've done a great deal of work in gathering and organizing your financial data, in fact you now have a perspective on your personal finances that most people will never achieve.

At this point, we've just gotta' find $200 per month in your spending plan. Anything above this is great but for now let's not stress, simply complete the following exercises and focus on finding that first $200.

Exercise 1: Needs vs. Wants

Begin by setting aside all worksheets and financial documents except your "Income Statement (Spending Plan)" worksheet.

This exercise is about taking a closer look at where you spend your money and placing each spending event into one of two categories: need or want. This process will help you to make better decisions with respect to your spending and take you one step closer to finding that $200 per month.

Needs are things that you absolutely couldn't do without. Examples would be mortgage / rent payments, food, transportation, etc. Wants are things that are nice and contribute to your lifestyle but if you really had to, you could give them up. Examples would be massages or spa treatments, gym memberships, premium cable television, expensive vacations, etc. Now review the entries on your Spending Plan worksheet and place an N next to the expenses that represent a need and a W next to the expenses that represent a want.

Once you have completed this labeling process go through the list a second time and ask yourself the following questions for each want:

- Could I do without this item if I really had to?
- Could I find a way to get the same result or level of satisfaction from this item in a way that costs less?

Now ask these questions for each need:

- Is there a way I can get this for less?
- Is there a way I can do this less often?
- Is there a less expensive option?

Once you have completed this process, add up the dollar amounts saved or eliminated and input the total on the line for "Possible Financial Freedom Payment" on the bottom right hand of the worksheet. If this number adds up to more than $200 congratulations! You are well on your way. If not, don't get discouraged, there are more ways to find this money in a later chapter.

Again, the goal of this exercise is to free up money from your cash flow that can be applied to your financial Freedom payment (FFP) each month to rapidly eliminate debt and build your wealth. You will learn more about the FFP and how to apply it in the next chapter but as a brief teaser, you will want to make sure that you apply the amount of any expenses you were able to reduce or eliminate directly to your monthly FFP so that it won't slip through another crack in your finances and be spent.

Real World Example:

When we work with clients on their spending plans we complete the "Income Statement (Spending Plan)" spreadsheet for them so they can get a clear picture of how money moves through their life. Many people don't have a clear idea of exactly how they plan to spend their money on a monthly basis let alone where it went in previous months.

This is not a budget exercise. This is a flexible spending plan that assists our clients in managing the most valuable financial asset most of them possess, the stream of income that comes from their earning ability. Depending on how you decide to spend it, your income can be used to enhance your lifestyle and build real wealth or it can drain out of your life in unproductive ways so that you wake up 10 years down the road in the same situation as today.

A while back we worked with a client named Mary. When we completed her Income Statement (Spending Plan)" worksheet, Mary had $290 each month going into the "other" category. "Other" is a catch-all category that represents unaccounted for spending that was basically leaking out of her bank account each month through unplanned and unconscious spending.

She also had very little money going into the joy category for things that make her feel good.

We walked Mary through the wants vs. needs exercise from the previous section and found all of the areas where Mary was spending money on wants that weren't truly enhancing her quality of life. We then reduced the amount of spending in these areas to a comfortable level that made sense to Mary and entered the new spending target in the "planned spending" column.

Then we asked Mary two key questions that will begin your second exercise:

Exercise 2: Spend Shifting

1. What is most important to you in life?

    a. Follow-up to this question, how does that make you feel?

2. What specifically has to happen for you to feel that way on a regular basis?

What we have found is that impulse spending is most often an attempt to fill a void in a person's life. Whether it's a lack of excitement, the need to nurture or pamper oneself, stress relief, etc. the impact on the finances is the same. In most cases, when an individual begins to fulfill their needs in other ways, the destructive spending stops.

The opposite of impulse spending is being too tight with personal finances. Punishing oneself either consciously or subconsciously by living for creditors, pinching every penny and abstaining from even the most basic comforts is just as destructive to personal wealth and happiness as spending too freely.

Either challenge, impulse spending or chronic penny pinching can be addressed by asking the two questions above and then directing energy and financial resources into high lifetime value activities. High lifetime value activities are things that over time contribute to one's health, well-being, joy, and satisfaction on a deep emotional level.

Take for example the action of going to a movie. Unless it is an extraordinarily moving film or you are an avid film buff, this activity is simply an entertaining way to distract yourself for a couple of hours and spend $15. You could also take that same $15 and two hours and attend a Yoga class. The Yoga class, in addition to entertaining you for 2 hours would also have these benefits; balancing your mind, restoring your body, relieving stress, connecting you to your spirit.

Of course not everyone would agree that the goals and benefits of Yoga practice are important or meaningful to them but the concept is the same regardless of the activity. It has been said that the quality of your life is directly proportional to the amount of time you spend engaging in high lifetime value activities and we agree with this concept.

When we asked Mary these questions we found that she had always wanted a dog. She had one as a child and remembered how much joy and love it had brought into the family. She also really loved to shop and get manicures and pedicures because it made her feel good about her appearance and seemed to enhance her experience of everything else she did. So we added these expenses to the planned spending column on the spreadsheet. Through this process, we also found an extra $100 that Mary could apply to her FFP to reduce her student loan debt.

The net result for Mary was an immediate improvement in the quality of her life. With no sacrifice or struggle she was able to reallocate her resources from something that didn't matter much to her, eating out, into manicures, pedicures, a new puppy, more money for clothes and we shaved 10 years and over $30,000 in interest payments off her student loans by adding an additional $200 per month to her financial freedom payment.

We call this concept spend shifting. By simply making the conscious choice to shift spending from low yield activities and outcomes to high yield activities and outcomes you have a remarkable ability to dramatically increase your overall quality of life.

Exercise 3: Keep a Spending Record
(Advanced Strategy)

Clarity about your money is very important in terms of how much you have, and how it moves through your life. Often times when people are not able to find the $200 by going through the first two exercises in this chapter it is because they began this process without a clear understanding of exactly where their money goes. It is not at all uncommon for clients to know how much they spend on rent or their mortgage, car payments, and other large utility payments but have no idea where the rest of their income goes on a monthly basis.

This exercise will take some time but it will provide you with a level of clarity about how money moves through your life that will astound you. It will lift the financial fog that surrounds your spending and reveal new ways to find that first $200 for your financial freedom payment.

The instructions are simple, all you have to do is write down everything you spend each day for 21 days. There's no magic to the number 21 other than if you multiply it by 17 you get just about one year's worth of expenses.

Here are some pointers to keep you on track:

- Carry a small spiral notebook and pen or a single notecard folded in half with you to record daily expenses.

- Record the date at the top of the page or notecard and list what you spent money on and exactly how much.

- Do it every day, if you forget or skip, your results will suffer.

- Record everything. From $.25 cents for a parking meter to $4.95 for coffee.

- Try to record the transaction right when you spend the money or at least as soon as possible afterward so you don't forget.

- Don't round. Record amounts to the penny.

- At the end of the week total up all of the spending from each category so you know how much was spent for the entire week. Be as specific as possible with the categories because this is how you will find your "extra money". HINT: www.Mint.com is a free website that can be a huge help in automating this process for you.

- Don't forget credit card spending or checks you write.

- Review your spending each week by category as a want or need. It's not uncommon to spot some surprises you didn't know about now that this information is clearly laid out in front of you.

SPECIAL NOTE: Many people have found that completing this exercise has produced some significant surprises. Missed ATM withdrawals, unplanned and unrecorded impulse purchases, over spending on groceries and entertainment are just a few of the common discoveries made during this exercise.

What to look for as you complete the steps in Chapter 3 to make sure you are on the right track

As you begin to implement the action steps listed in the

following section, here's what to watch for to make sure that that you are on the right track:

- You should begin to see areas where you can cut or reduce spending.

- You should get a better feel for how money is moving through your life.

- You should begin to see opportunities to shift your spending from low value activities to high lifetime value activities.

- If you are not able to find at least $200 after completing the first two exercises, move on to the third and keep a spending record for 21 days.

Chapter 3 Action Steps Review

1. EXERCISE 1: Take out your completed Income Statement (Spending Plan) worksheet.

2. Go down each column and review every expense item marking an N for need or W for want next to each one.

3. Review each item marked W and decide which expenses can be reduced or eliminated from your spending plan altogether.

4. Total all eliminated and reduced amounts and enter that number on the possible financial freedom payment line.

5. EXERCISE 2: Ask yourself the spend shifting lifetime value questions:

   o What is most important to you in life?

- Follow-up to this question, how does that make you feel?
  o What specifically has to happen for you to feel that way on a regular basis?

6. With the answers to these questions in mind go through the wants expenses one more time to see which of these can be shifted to higher lifetime value activities.

7. EXERCISE 3: if you still have not found $200 or you want to increase your financial freedom payment to accelerate your pay off and save more money, begin keeping a spending record.

8. Obtain a small spiral notebook or deck of 3X5 index cards.

9. Each day for 21 days write the date on the top of one sheet or one 3X5 index card and record each time you spend money that day.

10. At the end of the week total all spending by category on a sheet of paper or use the Weekly spending record found in Chapter 7.

11. At the end of the month, if you decide to continue this valuable exercise (highly recommended) complete the monthly record found in Chapter 7.

12. Continue to monitor each spending category on a weekly basis. Be specific with the categories and notice large expenditures and areas where you could cut back.

Exercise 1

Take out completed Income Statement (Spending Plan) worksheet.

Mark each expense item with an N for need or W for want.

Review each expense item marked W and decide which expenses can be reduced or eliminated.

Total all eliminated and reduced amounts and enter that number on the possible financial freedom payment line.

Ask yourself the spend shifting lifetime value questions:

- What is most important to me in life?
  - How does that make me feel?

What specifically has to happen for me to feel this way on a regular basis?

Review wants expenses to see which ones can be shifted to higher lifetime value activities.

Exercise 3

Obtain a small spiral notebook or deck of 3X5 index cards.

For 21 days write the date on the top of one sheet or one 3X5 index card and record each time you spend money.

At the end of the week total all spending by category on a sheet of paper or use the weekly spending record found in Chapter 7.

At the end of the month, complete the monthly spending record found in Chapter 7.

Continue to monitor each spending category on a weekly basis to find areas where you could cut back.

Chapter 4: Take Action

Here's where the Rubber Meets the Road

"I've been paying for 7 years nonstop and I have only paid down $2,000.

You've accomplished a lot so far. You have found all of your financial documents, input the key information into worksheets so you could gain a clear picture of your financial situation, and you found money in your spending plan to apply to your financial freedom payment. Now you will pull everything together and concentrate the full power of your plan on eliminating your student loan debt faster than you ever thought possible.

If you learn and apply what I am about to teach you in this section, you will see your student loan debt balances falling rapidly each month, you will save thousands of dollars in interest payments, and you will shave up to 15 years off your original loan payment schedule. If you don't apply the information in this section, you will continue to be frustrated by student loan balances that continue to grow larger or if they do fall, they do so at a snail's pace despite your best efforts to pay them down.

Albert Einstein and Toxic Debt

"I'm stressed out because I can only pay the minimums each month."

According to the Cambridge dictionary, toxic debt is:

"Debt that has little chance of being paid back or of being paid back with interest, or an asset of which this is true."

Many people who are dealing with student loan debt have had the unfortunate   experience of coming out of a forbearance period and seen their loan balances skyrocket because the interest on their loans continued to accrue even though they weren't making payments. Others who are on an income driven or graduated repayment program continue to make payments but the lower monthly payments make far less impact on the outstanding loan balance which continues to add more and more interest to the account each month. This makes it seem as if you are not making any progress at all.

Basically anytime you see your loan balances going up or stagnating, you are in a toxic debt situation. As you saw from the definition above, this situation is very dangerous because as debt balances rise they can get out of control and become harder and harder to pay off. The longer it takes to pay debt off the more interest you pay and the less wealth you accumulate for yourself over your lifetime. This situation also robs you of your choices and options until the debt is paid back.

This brings us to the purported quote by Albert Einstein "Compound interest is the greatest invention in human history." Compound interest is basically a financial operation where accrued interest is added to the principal of the loan so that the added interest earns more interest. For an idea of the power of compounding, consider this story:

Two friends meet on the golf course and decide to wager on the round they are about to play. The cleverer of the two golfers suggests a wager of 10 cents on the first hole which will double on each hole thereafter. The second golfer agrees and they begin playing. The first hole is ten cents, the second is twenty and the third is forty, so far so good. Half way through at the ninth hole they were at $25.60 and things start to get interesting. The tenth hole is $51.20, the eleventh hole is $102.40 and the twelfth hole is $204.80. By the fourteenth hole things really accelerate as the bet reaches $819.20. This continues until the eighteenth hole where the bet reaches an astounding $13,107.20!

As you can see from this example compounding can be very powerful and it accelerates as the numbers get bigger. Well unfortunately the same concept also applies to your student loan debt. Thankfully your interest rate doesn't double every period (that would be a 100% interest rate) but it's important to remember that interest on your debt is working against you every hour of every day. Interest is like rust and like the old commercials for Rust-Oleum use to say, "Rust never sleeps."

So what's the solution? The first step is to pay at a minimum, all of the accrued interest each month on each loan so that it doesn't get added to principal and grow. The second step is to hammer down the *principal* balance as quickly as possible so that it generates less interest which in turn allows you to pay less interest and more toward principal each month in an upward momentum cycle.

What to do Right Now

"How do I get my budget together?"

Start by taking out your Debt Pay Off Order worksheet. Make the commitment to pay *only* the minimum monthly payment on each loan / debt on your worksheet with the following exception: the #1 pay-off priority loan / debt from column 5.

For the #1 pay off priority loan / debt, you will pay the monthly minimum *plus* the financial freedom payment amount you found in the last chapter and any extra you can afford in a separate check earmarked for principal only. IMPORTANT: Use the "Principal Payment Coupon" from Chapter 7 when you submit the extra payment.

Use this principal payment coupon anytime you want to make additional principal payments on your student loans or other secured debt (this coupon will not apply to unsecured debt like credit cards or store charge cards). Remember, this coupon should be used *only* for your #1 debt in the pay-off order.

Write two checks, one for the minimum payment and one for your financial freedom payment (FFP) amount for that month. Staple the minimum payment check to your regular payment coupon and staple the financial freedom payment check to this completed principal payment coupon. It is important to use this coupon to inform the lenders that your extra payment is to be applied to reduce the principal balance not subsequent interest payments. Lenders like to play games if you are not clear with your instructions and as you might imagine, the games they play benefit them, not you.

At the beginning of each month take a few minutes to plan where your money will go including the extra financial freedom payment which will be applied to your #1 priority loan / debt.

Hint: Your previous months spending record is a very helpful guide for this process.

This process will create a spending plan for you that will guide your monthly spending decisions in advance of their actual occurrence. One of the biggest leaks in a family's personal finances comes from unplanned spending. When a spending plan is created in advance of the money coming in, the chances of financial leaks goes down substantially and the chances of accomplishing what is really important to you goes up significantly.

If you follow this spending plan system along with the financial freedom payment and the principal payment coupon, you will see your #1 priority loan balance shrinking each month.

If you are very diligent with the system and apply the entire financial freedom payment plus the old #1 priority loan / debt payment to the #2 priority loan / debt once the priority #1 loan / debt is paid off, you will save yourself 10's of thousands of dollars in interest payments and shave over a decade off the time it will take to be completely debt free (based on a $100,000 loan / debt balance).

Case study for clarification of the process

Debt Pay-Off Order				
Name of Debt	Total Balance	Monthly Minimum Payment	Division Answer for Pay-Off Priority	Pay-Off Priority
ACS	$14,931.65	$325.00	46	1
Access Group	$7,400.87	$70.00	106	4
Sallie Mae 1	$4,628.22	$51.67	90	3
Sallie Mae 2	$85,289.31	$114.61	744	5
Visa	$4,522.00	$90.22	50	2
Totals				
1	2	3	4	5

Let's take a closer look at the completed sample client debt pay off order worksheet above and use it to clarify the process.

To begin, this client would pay the minimum balances from column 3 on each listed debt.

Any extra available cash would be added to the financial freedom payment and would be applied to the #1 debt. In this case it would be the ACS student loan found by taking the smallest balance from column 4 and ranking them in column 5.

If you receive any "found" money. That is: gifts, raises at work, tax refunds, or unexpected income, apply 50% of this new money to your #1 debt to increase your financial freedom payment for that month. If the increase is permanent, for example in the case of a raise, permanently increase your monthly financial freedom payment by 50% of the amount of the increase in your income and then incorporate the remaining 50% into your normal monthly spending plan.

Once the ACS student loan is paid off, apply the minimum payment of the ACS loan - $325 to the financial freedom payment for the #2 debt which is the Visa credit card balance.

This payment will be in addition to the normal monthly Visa payment and any previous financial freedom payment you have been able to free up from chapter 3. The new Visa monthly payment will look like this:

Visa monthly minimum payment = $90.22

Plus

ACS monthly minimum payment (once paid off, now rolls over into your financial freedom payment) =$325

Plus

Financial freedom payment (cash freed up from spending plan, for illustration purposes) = $200

51

Equals

The new monthly payment for the #2 debt, Visa = $615.22

Remember that any additional payments above the monthly minimum for your #1 debt must be sent in with a separate check accompanied by the principal payment coupon (see Chapter 7). Use these coupons to make additional principal payments on your student loans or other secured debt. **NOTE:** These coupons should be used only for your current #1 debt in the pay-off order. Write two checks, one for the minimum payment and one for your FFP amount for that month. Staple the minimum payment check to your regular payment coupon and staple the FFP check to one of these completed coupons.

As you can see from the above chart, any additional cash flow you allocate toward your FFP each month will have a dramatic impact on the total interest you pay and the amount of time it takes for you to be debt free.

What to look for as you complete the steps in Chapter 4 to make sure you are on the right track

As you begin to implement the action steps listed in the following section, here's what to watch for to make sure that that you are on the right track:

- You should begin to see the dramatic impact that additional focused principal payments will have on your pay off schedule.

- You should begin to feel more confident because you have a clear plan and you are taking action on the exact steps that will accelerate your loan pay off.

- When you sit down to pay your bills, you should not experience the sense of dread and anxiety because now there is clarity in your finances.

Chapter 4 Action Steps Review

1. Take out the completed debt pay off order spreadsheet.

2. Consult your monthly spending record for last month and create a spending plan for this month.

3. Identify your financial freedom payment.

4. Print the principal payment coupon from Chapter 7.

5. Pay the minimum balances on each debt.

6. For the #1 pay off priority debt write an additional check for the financial freedom payment and staple it to the completed principal payment coupon.

Take out debt pay off order spreadsheet.

Review last months spending record and create new spending plan.

Identify financial freedom payment.

Print principal payment (PP) coupon from website or copy from chapter 7.

Pay the minimum balances on each debt.

For #1 pay off priority debt write additional check for the financial freedom payment and staple it to completed PP coupon.

Chapter 5: Monitor Progress

Make Failure Impossible

"What's the fastest and easiest way to pay off my student loans and still be able to eat and live?"

Nice work! Just to recap all you have accomplished, take a look at this: you have found all of your financial documents, input the key information into worksheets so you could gain a clear picture of your financial situation, found money in your spending plan to apply to your financial freedom payment, and most importantly, you put your plan into action. Now you will learn how to stay on track and continue to produce results right up to the point where you are completely debt free.

As you begin this new process you may have a tendency to slip back into old habits that won't help you to reach your goals. That's where momentum comes in.

If you follow the steps outlined in this chapter you will: stay motivated, make consistent measurable progress toward paying off all of your debt including student loans, you will feel better about your finances and your enjoyment of life will improve immediately and it's also common for unexpected positive events to occur once you have committed to this plan. We have seen some pretty amazing and unexplainable things happen to clients like opportunities to make more money, or sudden windfalls occur once they had a good plan in place and were out of the fear surrounding student loan debt and their personal finances.

What You Measure, You can Manage

"I paid off the smaller loans because I thought it would make me

feel better. It didn't."

How many times have you tried to build a new habit? Whether it's losing weight, starting an exercise program, or spending more time with the family the hardest part is the beginning when the actions are new and you haven't gotten them ingrained into your schedule as habits.

Psychologists tell us that there are four stages involved in learning any new skill:

1. Unconscious incompetence – This is where we don't know that we don't know. In the context of this program this would be a situation where someone doesn't know that the strategy they are using to pay off student loan debt isn't efficient and they had no idea that there was a better way so they keep on doing what they are doing and receiving dismal results.

2. Conscious incompetence - This is where we know that we don't know. In the context of this program this would be the point where someone realizes that there is a better way to achieve the results they want. They don't know what the steps are but they do know that someone has figured out a better way to approach the student loan debt problem.

3. Conscious competence – This is where we know that we know. An example would be someone who has completed this program, knows the steps to take to get a better result. And can follow those steps by consciously focusing on the tasks and by reviewing the material when necessary.

4. Unconscious competence – This is where we don't know that we know. At this stage, the new skill has been mastered to the point where it can be completed without conscious focus and attention to the specific details. The

skill becomes internalized and is performed as if it were second nature with little conscious attention.   For another good example of unconscious competence take a moment and remember yourself tying your shoes this morning. If you can barely remember the action but your shoes are firmly tied, that's what unconscious competence is all about.

Let's go back to the puzzle analogy for a moment. At this stage all of the preliminary actions have been taken, you have dumped out the pieces, organized them by color and shape, built the frame of the picture and have begun working on one of the prominent images in the picture based on the cover of the box. Now imagine that your puzzle has 100,000 pieces. Even if you are doing everything right, progress may seem painfully slow as you compare your seemingly meager progress to the completed puzzle. This is where you need some help to keep you motivated and on track until the actions become automatic.

There is a simple four-step process that will significantly increase your probability of success in achieving any new goal.

1. Simple recognition of the truth

2. Make the process fun

3. Get accountability

4. Baby steps

Simple recognition of the truth

Now that you have your Balance Sheet (Net Worth Statement) prepared you have a very clear picture of where you are starting your journey on the way to debt freedom. This worksheet can do two powerful things for you, when you look at the number it can motivate you to find more money for your financial freedom payment each month and it can also serve as a baseline, a point of comparison with which you will gage your progress.

In Tim Ferriss' book *The Four Hour Body*, he shares the true story that beautifully illustrates the power of simple awareness and the effect that it can have on meeting your goals.

Phil Libin, who at the time weighed 258 pounds, wanted to lose weight but like many people he had tried diet and exercise on and off for years with spotty results. So rather than start another fad diet or exercise program, he decided to try an experiment to see whether he could accomplish his goal by making just one change: simply becoming more aware of his weight.

Phil created a spreadsheet with a graph showing his starting weight at one end and his goal weight of 230 at the other end, with a line between the two. Above and below the line he drew boundary lines. He knew that his weight probably wouldn't follow the line exactly from the starting weight to the goal weight but he reasoned that if he could stay between the top and bottom boundary lines he would be able to make sure he was proceeding in the right direction and remain on track.

At this point, all Phil had to do was track his weight from day to day and enter it into the spreadsheet. If his weight fell below the bottom line at any point, he would eat more. If his weight went above the top line, he would eat less.

The most startling part of this experiment was that Phil made no other attempt to change his behavior. He didn't exercise, try a new diet, or consciously change anything with respect to his weight except monitor it. Long story short, he ended up exactly where he intended to be at the end of the six month experiment, at his target weight of 230 pounds.

Phil's experience makes a strong case for awareness and the

recognition of truth being not only an important prerequisite for other desired life changes, but a force for change on its own. Also, it makes a good case for focus: if all you need to focus on to achieve your goal is to "stay between the lines," then it becomes much easier to stay mentally on task.

Another quick example of how simple recognition of the truth can help you meet your goals comes from the Body-For-Life Challenge, one of the largest physique transformation contests in history. Although the finalists for this contest employed a wide variety of different diet and exercise methods, the one thing that was almost unanimously credited with giving the contestants the motivation to stick with the program was the "before" photo they took of themselves.

The before photos were often place in a spot where they couldn't be ignored like the refrigerator and served as a daily reminder of what they were trying to accomplish and the consequences for self-sabotage.

Your Balance Sheet (Net Worth Statement) is your baseline. It is your before picture. Refer to it frequently, measure your progress and stay motivated to see that net worth number grow.

Make the process fun

As humans, we have been playing games since our first appearance here on earth. There is something inherently captivating about playing games and the desire to excel at the tasks required in playing them well. Watch any child with a video game and you will quickly see that there is focus, concentration, and exhilaration when a new skill is mastered or a new level is achieved.

As a society we spend an incredible amount of time and energy playing games. From sports, to gambling, to video games, to crossword puzzles, we all seem to have a particular game that interests and captivates us for hours on end.

What is it that motivates us to spend hours on that golf swing or an evening in front of the computer playing World of Warcraft? More importantly, is there a way to bottle up this motivation we have to excel at our chosen game and apply it to our financial life?

Donald Clark with Caspian Learning has an answer for what makes us motivated. He says that our motivation breaks down into 7 factors.

1. Motivation is more effective when it is intrinsic.

2. There must be autonomy.

3. Self-confidence and self-belief matter.

4. Challenge is important.

5. Goals are key.

6. Feedback is necessary.

7. Social approval by people who matter to you is important.

INTRINSIC

Contrary to popular belief, it is motivation that changes behavior long-term not willpower. Motivation is what stirs you to action and regulates your behavior and its origin comes from two sources, intrinsic (from within) and extrinsic (from without).

Intrinsic is the stronger of the two and it arises from within through reflection, from a natural interest, or from curiosity.

Extrinsic motivation as the name would imply comes from an external source such as: approval from family, society or peers. The desire for reward, monetary and other. And the threat of negative consequences, jail, pain, deadlines, surveillance, etc.

Long-term the strongest and most effective motivator comes from within and is self-generated.

AUTONOMY

Motivation is always stronger and the chances of follow-through are greater when the choice is made by the actor. When people feel like they made the choice themselves to engage in a specific action their buy in creates ownership of the game and produces a fuller participation and engagement. If you feel confident, in control and that you are making your own choices you feel better overall with the process.

SELF CONFIDENCE

Belief in your own ability to produce results from your efforts is a critical component to making games fun. If you don't believe that you can make a difference in your situation, then you won't even try.

There are several ways to increase self-confidence: build references, remember times in the past where you were successful at something. Accomplish small tasks that are challenging and meaningful so you can gain momentum.

CHALLENGE

When we are being challenged our attention and focus is engaged and enhanced.

GOALS

Motivation for any achievement begins with goals. Learning any new skill or activity will require a large amount of trial and error. What keeps you going when times are tough? It is a big why. The reason why you are doing a task is always linked to something you are trying to create in the future. If that thing you want in the future is the center of your focus and it's big enough and compelling enough, then short-term hardship is easier to endure.

The old saying practice makes perfect is not quite accurate. It is more accurate to say, "Perfect practice makes perfect." Simply doing something over and over will not help you get better at it. Doing a task or activity with specific attention to the outcome then changing your behavior to produce the desired result is how mastery is obtained.

SOCIAL APPROVAL

Human beings are very motivated by the approval of others that matter to them. From their peer groups, to family and friends if they are able to do something that elicits a favorable response from those they care about it produces a feeling of well-being.

Get accountability

The biggest mistake people make in trying to change any habit or learn any new skill is to rely on willpower. Studies have shown again and again that our will power is a limited resource and becomes depleted quite quickly as we go through a normal day.

Does this scenario sound familiar? Your alarm clock goes off in the morning and you force yourself to get up even though you really would like to catch a few more minutes of sleep. You force yourself to do some stretching because you know it's the right thing to do then you hop in the shower and get dressed. You skip the eggs and bacon in favor of the "healthy" breakfast options because your doctor said it's the best thing to do. At the office you struggle to pay attention during several long meetings, avoid the chocolate cake that someone left in the break room, skip the burger in favor of a salad at lunch, force yourself to make several unpleasant phone calls and complete that report that you have been putting off for a week.

Is it any wonder that by the time you get home all you feel like doing is grabbing the remote and flipping channels on the TV? You have spent all day depleting your willpower by forcing yourself to do things that you would rather not do and when you finally make it home your willpower muscle is exhausted.

Studies have also shown that every additional decision people are required to make reduces physical stamina, their ability to perform numerical calculations, persistence in the face of failure and overall mental focus.

Hopefully by now you realize that relying on willpower to change behavior long-term is a losing battle. That is where habit steps in.

Baby steps

So what's the solution? The solution is to create a new habit that incorporates your desired behavior. One way to accomplish this is by making small temporary changes that are linked to existing habits. Stanford professor BJ Fogg has done extensive research on how habits are formed and he has found the following; if you can create a series of tiny habits, no more than 3 per week, that take less than 30 seconds to complete, and then link them to an existing habit like waking up, or going to the bathroom or brushing your teeth, then you can train yourself to adopt not only these small habits but other bigger more life changing habits in the future.

Another way to change behavior is to remove the barriers that prevent you from accomplishing the desired behavior or conversely, you can increase barriers to prevent yourself from doing things that you find destructive.

In order to understand how this works you need to understand a concept of activation energy. Activation energy is the energy required to complete a task or the barrier between you and an activity. Shawn Achor gives a great personal example of activation energy in his book The Happiness Advantage. Shawn Achor is a Harvard trained positive psychologist and he was eager to implement the advice of the late Harvard alum, William James in developing a habit of practicing his guitar every day.

He decided to make a spreadsheet with 21 columns one for each of the 21 days that common wisdom tells us it takes to develop a habit. Three weeks later he looked at the grid in disgust because only the first 4 boxes were checked off. After analyzing the situation he realized that it was the simple 20 seconds of activation energy of walking to the closet and taking out the guitar that stood between him and the new habit. At the end of the 4th day his willpower to overcome these 20 seconds of extra effort had simply been depleted.

What he did next was purchase a $2 guitar stand and set it up in the middle of his living room. He then repeated the experiment successfully with 21 straight days of checkmarks. The only thing that changed was that he put his desired behavior on the path of least resistance. That simple 20 extra seconds to walk over and take out the guitar was all that stood between him and successfully practicing every day.

What to Do Right Now

"I've paid a lot and the loan balances are not going down."

Legendary Harvard psychologist William James said that human beings are, "mere bundles of habits." Changing your existing money habits may be challenging at first but here's how to use what you've learned in this chapter about motivation and momentum to change your behavior and create the results you want.

We want to create the habit of monitoring your net worth and the balance of your # 1 loan / debt each month so you can see progress. When you see the balance on your #1 loan / debt falling fast it will give you the encouragement you need to follow through with the plan you have developed and pay off all of your debt fast.

You can remind yourself to monitor these numbers by marking it in your calendar or you can set up an automatic reminder using Cozi.com. On this site you can set up recurring reminders via email or text sent directly to your mobile phone that keep you on track.

If you want a friend to help you stay on track, you can both sign up for Stickk.com. This site will help you create a goal and accountability toward accomplishing that goal in the form of a referee and supporters who are kept apprised of your progress.

In order to monitor these numbers you will have to repeat the steps in chapter 1 and 2 each month or take a shortcut.

The Short Cut

Mint.com – Mint is a free website with bank-level security that pulls all of your financial accounts and transactions into one place so you can get a big picture view of what your money is doing. You can set up your spending plan, establish and track goals, monitor cash flow and your net worth in real time with the push of a button.

Once you have set your account up with Mint.com, all of your accounts will be automatically updated with the most current information each time you log-in. This will allow you to access your net worth each month with a few mouse clicks. You can also do the same for your #1 loan / debt in the payoff order.

Once you have obtained these numbers from Mint.com each month, record them on the Momentum Tracking Worksheet from Chapter 7. Accomplishing this task will give you tangible proof that your plan is working as you see that your net worth is increasing and your #1 pay off priority debt is decreasing dramatically each month.

What to look for as you complete the steps in Chapter 5 to make sure you are on the right track

As you complete the steps in Chapter 5 you should see your net worth going up each month as you record the updated numbers on your momentum tracking worksheet. You should also see your #1 pay off priority debt going down substantially as you apply your financial freedom payment to the outstanding principal and record the new outstanding balance on your Momentum Tracking Spreadsheet.

Chapter 5 Action Steps Review

1. Set a monthly reminder to update your Momentum Tracking Worksheet.

    o Personal calendar

    o Cozi.com

2. Print out Momentum Tracking Worksheet from Chapter 7.

3. Input data into Mint.com (optional but a serious time saver).

4. Gather data for input into the worksheet.

   ○ Repeat steps in Chapters 1 and 2 each month.

   ○ Input data from Mint.com.

5. Complete the worksheet.

6. Celebrate your success.

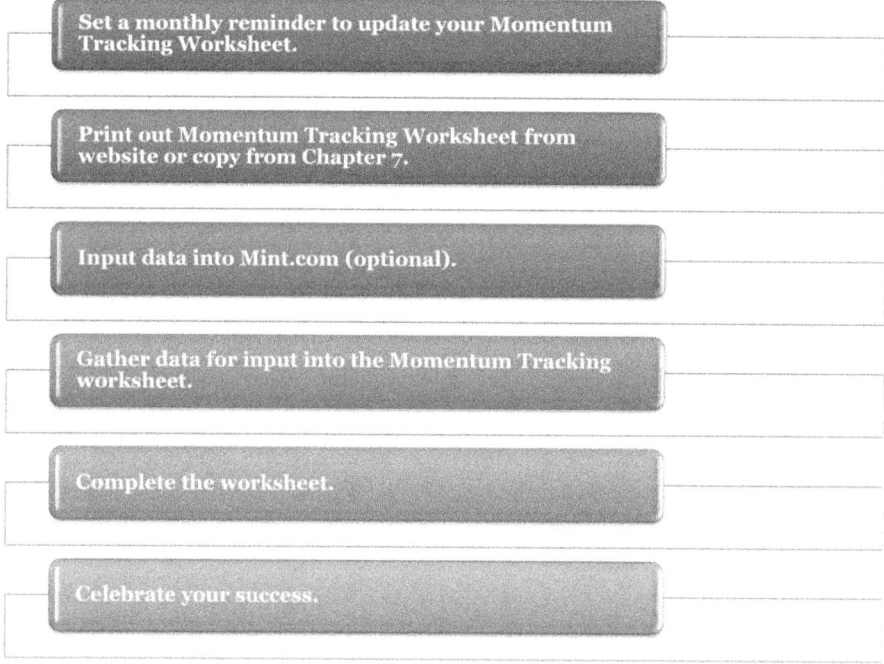

Set a monthly reminder to update your Momentum Tracking Worksheet.

Print out Momentum Tracking Worksheet from website or copy from Chapter 7.

Input data into Mint.com (optional).

Gather data for input into the Momentum Tracking worksheet.

Complete the worksheet.

Celebrate your success.

Chapter 6: Additional Resources

Help with Building a Student Loan Debt Elimination Plan / Webinars / Seminars / Private Consultation

http://financialevolutiongroupblog.com/

Student Loan / Personal Finance Tracking

www.Mint.com

(Mint does all the work of organizing and categorizing your spending for you. Set and track goals and monitor progress.)

www.ReadyForZero.com

(A simple way to control and reduce debt on-line)

www.Tuition.io

(A tool for managing student loans that lets you optimize your debt.)

www.LearnVest.com

(Create a budget, track spending, and monitor progress.)

Student Loan Information

www.EqualJusticeWorks.org

(Free educational debt webinars, articles, and resources.)

www.LoanConsolidation.ed.gov

(Information and application for Federal Direct Consolidation Loans.)

www.StudentLoans.gov

(Primary resource for Federal student aid.)

www.FinAid.org

(Student loan information, loan calculators, Q&A.)

www.NSLDS.ed.gov

(National Student Loan Data System. Retrieve your Federal student loan information.)

www.IBRinfo.org

(Independent, Non-profit source of information about new federal student loan payment and forgiveness programs.)

www.StudentAid.ed.gov

(U.S. Department of Education. Loan repayment calculators, Deferment and forbearance information, resolving disputes, Forgiveness, cancellation and discharge information.)

Student Loan Forgiveness Programs

www.SponsorChange.org

(Provides non-profits a way to recruit skilled college graduates to complete service projects. The graduates are compensated by sponsors in the form of student loan payments. Only available in Pittsburgh, PA for now.)

www.charityfordebt.wordpress.com/about/

(Non-profit dedicated to helping students by paying $15 per hour directly to pay back student loan costs when they volunteer for local charitable organizations. Only in Washington D.C. for now.)

www.studentaid.ed.gov/repay-loans/forgiveness-cancellation/charts/public-service

(Information on the federal Public Service Loan Forgiveness program.)

WWW.STUDENTAID.ED.GOV/REPAY-LOANS/FORGIVENESS-CANCELLATION/CHARTS/TEACHER

(Information on the federal Teacher Loan Forgiveness program and Teacher Cancellation program.)

www.americorps.gov/for_individuals/faq/index.asp#ccraa

(Often referred to as the "domestic Peace Corps" AmeriCorps coordinates domestic team-based service projects in five different areas-- natural and other disasters, infrastructure improvement, environmental stewardship and conservation, energy conservation, and urban and rural development-in communities in all 50 states and U.S. territories. Members receive a small bi-weekly stipend, food, lodging, and uniforms. Since the assignments are fulltime and the stipends modest,

AmeriCorps members are considered low income and are eligible for the IBR program. AmeriCorps service is also recognized as equivalent to a public service job for the purposes of the Public Service Loan Forgiveness program.)

www.equaljusticeworks.org/ed-debt/students/loan-repayment-assistance-programs/federal-LRAPs/JRJ

(The John R. Justice Student Loan Repayment Program (JRJ) provides loan repayment assistance for state and federal public defenders and state prosecutors.)

www.hrsa.gov/loanscholarships/repayment/nursing/

(Information on the Nursing Education Loan Repayment Program.)

Help for Student Loan Issues You Haven't Been Able to Resolve Through Your Lender

www.StudentLoanBorrowerAssistance.org

(A resource for borrowers that want to know more about their options and rights.)

WWW.STUDENTAID.ED.GOV/HOME

(For Federal student loan issues, search for ombudsman.)

WWW.CONSUMERFINANCE.GOV/OMBUDSMAN/

(Private student loan issues.)

www.house.gov/representatives/find/

(Your congressman/woman can also be a big help.)

Financial Calculators

www.Free-Online-Calculator-Use.com

(137 free on-line financial calculators.)

www.SmartAsset.com

(Interactive home buying guide shows you everything from how much you can afford, to how your taxes will change after buying and real mortgages you could qualify for. You can also use this site anonymously so it doesn't track your information.)

Investing

www.FutureAdvisor.com

(Personalized recommendations to optimize all of your investments including your 401(k).)

Saving Money

www.SaveUp.com

(Rewards program to help save money and get out of debt)

www.PetersFlights.com

(Cheap flights, hotels, and car rental)

www.SmarterBucks.com

(Rewards program for paying down student loans)

www.Stretcher.com

(Learn how to live better for less.)

www.CheapAir.com

(Cheap flights, hotels, car rental, and cruises.)

www.Orbitz.com

(Cheap flights, hotels, car rentals, and destination activities.)

www.Travelocity.com

(Cheap flights, hotels, car rental, and cruises.)

www.Kayak.com

(Cheap flights, hotels, car rental, and deals.)

www.Expedia.com

(Cheap flights, hotels, car rental, cruises, and activities.)

www.Ebates.com

(Merchants pay Ebates to refer customers to them. Ebates then pays a chunk of that back to you when you shop on their site.)

www.PerkStreet.com

(Get up to 5% cash back on your everyday purchases with the PerkStreet debit card and checking account.)

www.WhiteFence.com

(Enter your street address and the site quickly lets you compare rates for cable, internet, phone, electric, natural gas, and more.)

www.BillCutterz.com

(This is a bill discount service. You send them your bills and they call your providers and negotiate better rates on your behalf. You then split the savings with them.)

www.Groupon.com

(Save 50% - 90% on just about anything you can imagine.)

www.Restaurant.com

(Get discount restaurant coupons online.)

www.entertainment.com

(Get discounts on tons of products and services.)

Credit Information

www.AnnualCreditReport.com

(Get a free copy of your credit report from all 3 bureaus)

Save for Children's College / Money for College

www.SavingForCollege.com

(Complete guide to saving for college)

www.GradSave.com

(College savings plan registry)

www.GreenNote.com

(Money for college from people who believe in you.)

www.Prosper.com

(Peer to peer lending. This site connects people who want to lend money to those who want to borrow it.)

www.FC2Success.org

(Scholarships and grants for children in foster care.)

Cyber-Begging and Other Creative Ways to Pay Off Student Loan Debt

www.LilysList.com

(Gift registry for anyone with student loans)

www.StudentLoanList.com

(Connects donors with student loan borrowers who need help)

www.EducationRegistry.com

(Gift registry for past, current or future educational costs)

www.Indiegogo.com

(Global crowd-sourcing platform for raising money for any type of campaign.)

www.MelodysDream.com

(Creative example of a good cyber-begging site.)

www.GoFundMe.com

(Crowd-sourcing platform for raising money on-line.)

Employment Information / Creative Ways to Earn Extra Money

www.Salary.com

(Search jobs and salary ranges by zip code.)

www.PayScale.com

(Compare your salary to a database of 35 million people covering 12,000 job titles 1,100 industries and 150 countries.)

www.Elance.com

(The world's leading site for online work.)

www.Odesk.com

(The world's 2nd largest online workplace.)

WWW.CRAIGSLIST.ORG

(Local online classifieds and forums - community moderated, and largely free.)

www.99Designs.com

(The fastest growing design marketplace in the world.)

www.Fiverr.com

(The world's largest marketplace for Small Services, Starting at $5.)

www.HubPages.com

(Hubbers (HubPages authors) earn money by publishing their Hubs (content-rich Internet pages) on topics they know and love.)

www.Squidoo.com

(Similar to HubPages, authors receive royalties for creating online content.)

www.FreeRangeStock.com

(Photographers receive royalties for posting their work online.)

Chapter 7: Forms

NOTE: You can find PDF copies of all of these forms on our website: http://financialevolutiongroupblog.com/

Document Checklist

Personal Financial Planning Documents

_____   Current Mortgage Statements for

all Real Estate

_____   Financial Statements (Include)

> Investment Statements (personal)
>
> 401(k) Statements
>
> ESOP
>
> Deferred Compensation
>
> Pension Projections
>
> College Savings Account (statements)
>
> Auto / RV Statement
>
> Other Liabilities (credit, equity line)
>
> Living Expenses Projections or Budget

(Quicken, Excel Reports)

_____ Checkbook Register, Check Stubs, or Check Copies for all Bank Accounts

_____ Credit Card Statements

_____ Savings and Checking Account Statements for all Accounts (last 3 months to get a feel for the trend, one month alone could be unusually high or low)

_____ Student Loan Statements (all)

_____ Personal Loan Information (can be a handwritten list of anything else you owe)

_____Pay stub from your employer(s)

_____Pension, disability / Social Security, or retirement income statements

_____Alimony or child support

Income Statement (Spending Plan Spreadsheet)

Spending Plan Worksheet

	Actual Spending	Planned Spending	Difference	N/W		Actual Spending	Planned Spending	Difference
Core Expenses (70%)					**Joy Expenses (10%)**			
Home Related					**Travel**			
-Mortgage / Rent Payment					-Vacations / All Associated Expenses			
-Garden Supplies					-Other			
- Property Insurance					-Other			
- Home Maintenance					**Entertainment / Hobbies**			
- Property Tax					-Cable TV			
-Home Repairs					-Internet			
-Home Security					-Video / DVD Rentals			
-Housecleaning Service					-Movies / Plays			
-Other					-Concerts / Clubs			
Food					- Club Dues / Health Club, Country Club, etc.			
- Groceries					- Recreation			
- Dining Out (other than work lunches)					- Pets / All Expenses, Food, Boarding, Vet. Etc.			
- Going out for lunch at work					- Subscriptions / Magazine, etc.			
Clothing					- Sports Equipment			
- Purchase					- Toys for Children			
- Dry Cleaning					- Other			
Healthcare or Medical					- Other			
- Insurance					- Other			
- Deductible					**Personal Care**			
- Prescriptions					-Massage / Spa / Manicure			
-Co-pays / Out of the Pocket					-Haircuts			
- Medications / Over the Counter					-Other			
Personal Debt Payment (minimum)					**Accumulation Expenses (10%)**			
Utilities					**Vacation Home**			
- Electricity/ Gas					**Boat**			
- Telephone					**Recreational**			
- Cell Phone					**College**			
- Water/ Sewer/ Garbage					**Savings**			
- Other					**Other**			
- Other					**Transition Of Wealth**			
- Other					**Heirs**			
- Other					**Charities**			
Insurance					**Gifts To Trust**			
- Long-Term Care					**Subtotal**			
- Life								
- Disability					Income	Client	Spouse	
- Other								
- Other					W2 Earnings (Job 1)			
Transportation					W2 Earnings (Job 2)			
- Car Payment					Pension			
- Insurance					Social Security			
- Fuel					Business Income			
- Maintenance / Repairs					Gifts			
-Car Wash / Detailing					Investment Income			
-Parking					Other			
-Public Transportation					Other			
Other Living Expenses					Total Income			
-Child Care					Possible Financial Freedom Pmt. (10%)			
-Other					Total Expenditures			
Subtotal					Monthly Income Availability			

Balance Sheet (Net Worth Statement)

Assets	Amount	Liabilities	Amount
Balance Sheet (Net Worth Statement)			
Taxable Accounts			
Cash Accounts		**Student Loans**	
- Checking	$		$
- Savings	$		$
- CD's	$		$
- Money Market	$		$
- Other	$		$
- Other	$		$
Investment Accounts			$
-Brokerage Account	$		$
-Mutual Fund Account	$		$
-Other	$		$
-Other	$		$
Qualified Accounts		**Credit Cards**	
- 401(k)	$		$
- 403(b)	$		$
- IRA	$		$
- Other	$		$
- Other	$		$
Tax-Deferred Accounts		**Auto Loans**	
- Annuity	$		$
-Other	$		$
Tax-Free Accounts		**Misc. / Personal Loans**	
- Roth IRA	$		$
- Tax-Free Bonds	$		$
- 529	$		$
- Education IRA	$		$
- Other	$		$
Real Property		**Mortgage**	
- Residence	$		$
- Real Estate	$		$
Life Insurance			
- Policy 1 Cash Value	$		
- Policy 2 Cash Value	$		
Non-Working Assets			
- Art/Jewelry	$		
- Automobiles	$		
- Other Personal Property	$		
Total Assets	$	**Total Liabilities**	$
NET WORTH (Assets - Liabilities)			$

Debt Pay Off Order Spreadsheet

Debt Pay-Off Order				
Name of Debt	Total Balance	Monthly Minimum Payment	Division Answer for Pay-Off Priority	Pay-Off Priority
Totals				
1	2	3	4	5

Weekly Spending Record

Weekly Spending Record								
Category	Monday	Tuesday	Wednesday	Thursday	Friday	Saturday	Sunday	Totals

Monthly Spending Record

Monthly Spending Record					
Category	Week 1	Week 2	Week 3	Week 4	Totals

Principal Payment Coupon

Apply this amount $ _____
Check # _____ to repay the balance of loan
_____
NOTE TO FINANCIAL INSTITUTION: Extra payment is to go on the
principal of the next (not the last) payment and sequential adjacent
payments until all of the extra payment is used.

Name(s) on Loan _____
Address _____
City _____ State _____
Zip _____

If you have questions, please call me
at _____ .

Momentum Tracking Worksheet

Momentum Tracking Worksheet		
	Net Worth	#1 Pay Off Priority Debt Balance
January		
February		
March		
April		
May		
June		
July		
August		
September		
October		
November		
December		

Special Bonus Chapter:99 Ways to Plug the Financial Leaks in Your Life and Find More Money for Your Financial Freedom Payment

The Little Leaks that Keep You Feeling Broke

In today's world there are so many things vying for our attention that it's easy to lose focus on what's really important. This is also true for our finances. From small impulse purchases that don't seem to matter to overpaying for a service here or a meal there all of these things add up and rob you of your lifetime wealth.

In this chapter you will find a list of practical, real world ways to save money and improve the quality of your life. Just remember so pass a little of that savings along to your financial freedom payment.

This is Not About Austerity

Remember, this system is not about basic survival. You are not trying to live a life in virtual poverty toiling for your creditors. Money is not math, it is emotion. Use these ideas that others have used with success as a springboard for coming up with your own solutions. You want to improve the quality of your life long-term and these are simply guidelines to help you pay off debt and build wealth in the fastest way possible.

The Tips

1. Barter or exchange services instead of paying in cash. Use your expertise in any area in exchange for someone else's that you need. Babysitting is a great example.

2. Collect a debt owed to you.

3. Collect back salary or wages.

4. Cancel an order and get your deposit back.

5. Go through the pockets in all of your clothes and your wallets and purses.

6. Request small cash gifts from relatives. (Gifts not loans.)

7. Enlist the help of your family to help with saving for your child's college education. If you open up a 529 plan, any family member can contribute and it makes birthday and holiday gift giving simple and meaningful. This will relieve the bulk of your burden for this expense and free up cash for your FFP until your debts have been paid off.

8. Stay home and watch TV instead of going out to a movie.

9. Entertain at home instead of taking people out.

10. Travel by train instead of plane.

11. Wear last year's clothes a little longer.

12. Purchase less and only buy items that are on sale

13. Get a hot water heater with a timer. Do you really need scalding hot water at 2AM?

14. Maintain your daily spending record.

15. Reduce the frequency of nonessential services, such as

lawn maintenance or consider doing them yourself.

16. Eat more meals at home instead of out.

17. Give gifts of personal service or things you have made by hand rather than buying them.

18. Borrow books, DVD's, etc. from the library rather than buying them.

19. Caulk, insulate and weather strip so you don't cool and heat the outdoors.

20. Close shutters and shades to cool your house in the summer and open them up to heat your house in the winter.

21. Buy clothes that can work with more than one outfit.

22. Make money with your clutter by selling it on ebay.com or Craigslist.org, Amazon.com or have a garage sale. If you do this online all you need is an account, snap a few digital pictures with your phone and wait for buyers to come to you.

23. Sign up for a class at a local community college and use your student ID to work out at the gym on campus. This can be much cheaper than a gym membership.

24. If you are still in school or going back, consider buying and selling your books on Amazon.com. It's possible to get your books for free this way.

25. Shop when no one else wants to. Go Christmas shopping in January and shop for a house or car in the rain. When you are shopping for a home the best time to buy is the dead of winter when everyone else wants to stay inside. Buying holiday cards, wrapping paper, decorations etc. just after the holidays will save you a bundle.

26. When you need a new appliance, send out an email to family and friends or just ask around. Also check on Craigslist.org and Freecycle.com.

27. Use grocery store club cards.

28. When dining out, skip the appetizers, desserts, and stick to soft drinks.

29. Buy in bulk.

30. Never shop on an empty stomach and always shop with a list. Skipping either of these steps will virtually guarantee you leave the store with a bunch of unnecessary junk food and snacks.

31. Remember that the store owners are cleaver; the most expensive items are usually stocked from waist to shoulder level. Going outside of this zone can often result in bargains for you.

32. Buying the store brand is fine. Often the store brands contain the exact same ingredients as the name brand and cost much less.

33. Skip convenience stores and gas stations for food shopping. All food items are marked up here.

34. Compare unit prices when shopping. Most items in stores now have a per unit price listed on the shelf under the product. This is an easy way to do an apples to apples comparison between two products that may be different sizes.

35. Don't fall for the floor plan tricks grocery stores play. The most frequently purchased items are always placed in the back of the store. Have you ever noticed that milk, eggs, and meat are never in the front of the store? The reason is that they know if they can get you to walk all

the way through the store there is a good chance you will pick up extra impulse items that you weren't planning on buying. And beware the checkout lines. They are loaded with impulse items that you don't need. Also notice how low the brightly colored candy is stocked in the check-out lines. Keep your small children in the cart to keep small hands from adding to your grocery bill.

36. Apply for a reduction in alimony or child support.

37. Give up a costly habit, such as smoking, coffee, snacking, shopping for fun (retail therapy) etc.

38. Use parks, high school and college tracks, hiking trails, and public recreation areas for sports and exercise instead of clubs or gyms.

39. Consider museums, galleries, and free public events for entertainment.

40. Repair damaged items rather than buy new ones.

41. Cut down the number of hours of household help (if you have this luxury).

42. Take in a border or roommate.

43. Don't keep your refrigerator or freezer as cold. Keep your freezer as full as possible to avoid cooling empty space. Use ice blocks if necessary.

44. Only run full loads of laundry and dishes to save water and energy.

45. Use lower flow shower heads and toilets.

46. Put in overtime at work.

47. Do private tutoring or consulting in an area of your

expertise.

48. Hold a garage sale.

49. Do temp or free-lance work. Check out www.elance.com
www.odesk.com , www.CraigsList.org ,
www.99designs.com , or www.Fiverr.com for ideas on
how people are making money in their spare time.

50. Use 50% of your tax refund to apply to your monthly FFP
for your #1 loan / debt in the pay-off order.

51. Use 50% of any cash gifts, or "found" money to apply to
your monthly FFP for your #1 loan / debt in the pay-off
order.

52. Split your raises at work. Use 50% of the amount of the
raise to increase your FFP and 50% of the amount of the
raise to allocate to items in your spending plan.

53. For any purchase over $100 use the "cool-off period".
Never buy the item the same day you see it. Instead
write the name of the item down along with the cost in
your calendar two days in the future. In most cases, after
48 hours the impulse to buy will have worn off. If you still
want the item and have room for it in your spending plan,
go ahead and purchase it.

54. Always ask for a discount.

55. Always use coupons and wait for sales.

56. Involve your entire family in the purchasing process.

57. Make it less convenient to spend money. Spend cash only
or designate specific times for shopping to reduce impulse
spending.

58. Handle emergencies and repairs immediately. This goes
for plumbing, auto, health, heaters, air conditioning etc.

If they aren't working properly they are costing you additional money each time you use them and often they are costing you money even when you aren't using them.

59. If you can, do it yourself. Cleaning, painting, basic maintenance. 70%-85% of a typical repair bill is labor. Save yourself this cost by checking on-line or borrowing a book from the library to complete these repairs yourself.

60. Skip the carpeting on your floor. The cost of cleaning and replacing the carpet can add up over the years.

61. Rent or borrow tools and appliances you will only use once or twice.

62. Get several bids on repair jobs you can't do yourself. Craigslist.org is a great place to start.

63. Cleaning sewer pipes and rain gutters on a regular basis will save you the hassle of expensive repairs down the line.

64. Buy energy efficient appliances and light bulbs.

65. Conserve energy. Turn lights out in rooms you are not in, set your thermostat a few degrees cooler in the winter and a few degrees warmer in the summer.

66. Shop at discount stores and factory outlets for clothes.

67. Look for irregular or imperfect clothing.

68. Don't be afraid to return items that don't perform as expected.

69. Off price stores can be a bargain. Ross, Burlington Coat Factory, TJ Maxx, and Marshalls buy last year's fashions in bulk and sell them at substantial discounts.

70. Buy out of season. Shop for your bathing suit in February

and your winter coat in July.

71. Never buy a new car. A new car will lose between 20% and 30% of its value when you drive it off the lot. If you really need the new car smell have them spray some the next time you have it washed. Consider off lease vehicles from the dealerships, buy from rental agencies, or buy used through a site like Craigslist.org. In addition, there are dozens of ways to purchase a quality used car through auctions. Here are a few to get you started:

o Classified ads

o Police Department

o County Sheriff's Office

o Highway Patrol

o IRS

o County Government

o Trustee Sales

o Probate Sales

o Estate Sales

o US Customs Service

o General Services Administration (GSA)

o Banks

o Credit Unions

72. If after all this you must have a new car, never finance it for longer than 36 months. Any longer and you will owe more than the vehicle is worth.

73. Carpool when possible.

74. Use public transportation if available.

75. Consider replacing cable with Netflix or RedBox. Unless you are a hyper consumer of TV you can replace a large percentage of these programs with lower cost alternatives including many free on-line options like Hulu.com.

76. Look for free or inexpensive outdoor entertainment. Do a Google search in your city to find dozens of options every day of the week.

77. Buy rush tickets for concerts and plays. 30 minutes before curtain you can often purchase tickets for events for substantial discounts. You can also check CraigsList.org for last minute deals on tickets and even find free deals.

78. Attend a book reading. View the on-line schedule for your local bookstore for details.

79. Don't automatically think that when you are bored you need to spend money. Think about high lifetime value activities like spending time with family, making a pleasurable phone call, taking a walk around a lake, or reaching for that book that you have been meaning to get to. Sometimes it's better to make the extra effort to entertain yourself rather than to fall back on spending money or reaching for technology to entertain us.

80. When purchasing electronics, simple is fine. Do you really need the extra bells and whistles?

81. Check fare sites like www.CheapAir.com , www.Orbitz.com , www.Travelocity.com , www.Kayak.com , or www.Expedia.com to find the best travel, airfare, and hotel deals.

82. Don't pay for anything but your room when staying at a hotel. Everything else is extremely expensive.

83. Consider vacationing close to home. If you have family that's fun to visit, this can save you even more money.

84. Consider camping. Camp grounds and RV parks offer some of the best views in the world and most are a fraction of the cost of a hotel stay.

85. Move into a smaller house, or apartment. If this makes sense for you particular situation it may be a way to save a significant amount of money.

86. Appeal your property tax. It never hurts to try.

87. Pay off your mortgage as quickly as possible. The longer you take to pay, the more interest you will eventually fork over.

88. Use direct deposit and automatic bill pay. This will make is easier to pay yourself first and reduce the possibility that you will make unplanned purchases.

89. Prepare your own taxes if you file a simple 1040 or 140EZ form. Turbo Tax is an amazingly simple piece of software that can save you $100's every year over hiring someone to do your simple tax returns.

90. Remember to take advantage of any student loan related tax credits or deductions you may qualify for e.g.:

    o The American Opportunity Scholarship (modification of the Hope credit)

    o The Lifetime Learning Credit

    o The Education Loan Interest Deduction

    o Check with your state to see if they offer any

additional tax credits or deductions.

91. Review insurance coverage. Raise deductibles where prudent and adjust coverage as necessary.

92. Contribute to your IRA or 401(k). This can give you an immediate tax break by reducing your taxable income.

93. Reconcile your bank statements. Yes, banks can and do make mistakes. Websites like www.Mint.com make this process much easier.

94. Don't pay late fees. Keep your finances organized to avoid late, over limit, and balance transfer fees. If you do get snagged, gather your records and give the financial institution a call to negotiate a fee waiver.

95. Keep a separate account for emergency expenses.

96. Host a garage sale.

97. Save your loose change.

98. Set reasonable spending limits for birthday and holiday gifts and stick to them.

99. For more ideas take a look at the web. Sites like www.Stretcher.com have hundreds more ideas on how to save money and make your financial life more efficient.

SPECIAL for Readers of *School Loans Gone*

Get More Help Paying Off Your Student Loans

Congratulations! You have just learned a very powerful and complete system to pay off all of your debt including your student loans. *School Loans Gone* is the result of over 18 years of meeting with clients one-on-one, reviewing and solving their challenges and seeing what really worked, in the real world, for real families.

That's a great start, but we are often contacted by readers who want more help or need to clarify certain aspects of the plan. Many of the calls and emails we receive are from people who have been making payments on their student loans diligently for years and are frustrated because no matter how much they pay, it never seems like they are making any real progress.

We have taken all of the frustrations, comments and suggestions our clients have shared with us over the years and combined them with the best real world practical solutions that have helped them to implement their plans, pay-off student loans fast and get back to enjoying their lives.

Benefits You Will Receive From Working with Us:

- How to make your student loan balances go down rapidly each month using the money you already earn. Even if you have been paying for years and have seen little or no progress.

- We show you the specific steps you need to take to get organized, gain confidence, and create a sense of possibility and momentum with your finances.

- How to maximize the biggest monthly payment you have besides rent to pay-off your debt fast (hint, it's

98

your student loan payment.)

- Exactly what to do to pay-off all of your debt including student loans without depriving yourself, long before you retire.

- The key to paying-off your student loans without giving up the other things you want to do such as: buying a house, saving for your children's college education or saving for your retirement.

- How to relieve the enormous financial stress on yourself and your marriage that the debt has created by knowing exactly what you have to do and the specific steps you need to take to get completely out of debt in the shortest possible time. No more guessing, worrying or wondering.

- The confidence of knowing that you have a flexible and workable plan that can be adjusted for any situation including a job loss, economic downturn, or other major event.

- A little known secret to get friends and family to help you save for your child's college education so you can focus your efforts on paying-off your own student loans before the kids start college.

- A simple tool to keep you organized financially and always on top of important documents.

In the past we have charged up to $9,000 to work personally with clients to develop a custom plan. For readers of *School Loans Gone*, we have decided to price this special service at $197 per 90 minute consultation. We will jump in and cover as much as possible in the first 60 minute call and then schedule a 30 minute follow-up call to review specific strategies and steps for implementation.

You get one-on-one attention, a customized personal analysis and recommendations based on our best secrets and techniques that will help you pay your student loans off fast. You will be guided step by step on exactly what to do and have access to ongoing support in maintaining momentum with your plan.

If you have a pretty good handle on your finances but would like a set of friendly eyes to look over your plan and make helpful suggestions, our FREE 20 minute consultation is an excellent option for you. Show up on the call with your documents and the #1 burning question that keeps you up at night and we will jump right in covering as much as possible on the call.

If for any reason you decide after we work together that this service is not for you, we will gladly refund 100% of your fee and let you keep any tools or spreadsheets we use in our analysis as your courtesy gift.

To get started simply:

- Send us an email at chris@FinancialEvolutionGroup.com

- Click the "Schedule an appointment" button on our website www.FinancialEvolutionGroup.com or

- Give us a call at 424-261-2825 and let us know you are ready to go.

We reserve special time slots for readers of *School Loans Gone* but they go fast. Contact us today and be on track for a bright financial future tomorrow.

www.ingramcontent.com/pod-product-compliance
Lightning Source LLC
Chambersburg PA
CBHW061514180526
45171CB00001B/174